Copyright 2023 by Tina Huỳnh. All rights reserved.
English translation copyright 2023 by Tina Huỳnh.

Songs used with permission.

Published by F-flat Books.

www.fflat-books.com

ISBN: **978-1-63991-146-2**

The Vietnamese Children's Songbook

Tina A. Huỳnh

Illustrated by Jessica Đinh

F-flat Books

For my parents

Table of Contents

Foreword..6
Preface..10
Vietnamese Pronunciation Guide...12
Vietnamese Children's Songs - Bài Hát Thiếu Nhi............................14
    Goin' Fishing – Chiều Nay Em Đi Câu Cá......................................16
    The Cat – Con Mèo..18
    The Toad – Con Cóc (Ra Mà Xem)...20
    Yellow Butterfly – Kìa Con Bướm Vàng...22
    The Two Little Lizards – Hai Con Thằn Lằn Con...........................24
    Look! There's An Elephant – Trông Kìa Con Voi...........................26
    The Little Stork – Mẹ Yêu Không Nào (Con Cò Bé Bé)................28
    Let's Get Our August Lanterns – Rước Đèn Tháng Tám................30
    Dad and Mom in the Rice Fields – Tía Má Em...............................32
Cultural Treasures: The Mid-Autumn Harvest Moon Festival - Tết Trung Thu.....34
    Mooncakes - Bánh Trung Thu..36
    Lanterns: How to Make a Lantern - Lồng Đèn................................40
    Let's Play a Game - Trò Chơi...42
    Map of Vietnam - Bản Đồ Việt Nam..44
    Let's Speak Vietnamese - Nói Tiếng Việt..45
About the Author and Illustrator...46
About the Contributing Artists..47
Audio Recording Track List...48

Foreword

In less than a half-century, multiple waves of Vietnamese-Americans have arrived to the United States with their language, their cultural histories, and their philosophical ideals that play out in their everyday lives. They came at the time of the Fall of Saigon at the close of the Vietnam-American War (1975), in their escapes by boat from the communist regime in the 1980s, and through the humanitarian arrangements since the 1990s for members of Vietnamese-American families, former prisoners, and Amerasian children. They live in Orange County, California (in cities like Garden Grove, Westminster, Santa Ana, and Anaheim), in San Jose, Houston, Philadelphia, Portland, Seattle, New York, and elsewhere across the country. Vietnamese-Americans are a vibrant weave in the American tapestry by now, a significant part of the American demographic whole even as they so uniquely color and influence it.

Today's Vietnamese-Americans have adapted to their new country even as they have shaped it, and many are second- and third-generation U.S. citizens. Still, Vietnamese cultural heritage is sustained and celebrated through various community events, language instruction for children, culinary preferences, and the embrace of extended families that include grandparents, aunts, uncles, and cousins. Festivals pay tribute to long-standing holidays such as Tết (the Lunar New Year), when parades and processionals happen in the community and at Buddhist temples and Catholic churches. Music features on holidays and at festivals, for recreation and entertainment, and for continuing a cultural identity that is reinforced by the sounds of their songs' language, melodies, and rhythmic nuances, and by the sounds of a wide array of traditional string, wind and percussion instruments. These sounds recall Vietnamese history and heritage, and connect people at a deep level to cultural knowledge and values.

Many Vietnamese-Americans are of two minds as they live their contemporary American lives while also honoring their ancestry, and upholding traditional cultural practices in new spaces that serve to bridge cultures.

From this backdrop of Vietnamese-American-ness comes *The Vietnamese Children's Songbook*, a rich repository of songs for children drawn from Tina A. Huỳnh's experiences as a Vietnamese-American child growing up in southern California. The collection's title is accurate, as it is truly a "cultural treasure" of songs. It is beautifully conceived by Dr. Huỳnh, a musician and educator, who was weaned on the Vietnamese songs that her parents would sing for her as a child. The songs are plentiful, playful, and powerful means of recalling childhood in a "Vietnamese accent", with mention of fishing for crabs, bamboo branches and palm trees, shining stars and star lanterns in the night, rice fields, full moons, festivals, and a menagerie of kittens, lizards, toads, elephants, spiders, storks, and butterflies. They feel culturally alive through the translations, descriptions of function and meaning, and suggestions for teachers and learners of musical and social interactions. The recordings of the songs bring them immediately to the ear, as they are sung and played (on guitar, flute and percussion instruments) by Vietnamese-American musicians who understand and thus convey the nuances of language and music. Additional to the songs themselves in this collection are descriptions of mooncakes as festival treats for Tết (the Mid-Autumn Harvest Moon Festival), and lanterns for children to make and carry in festival processions. There is also description of a notable children's hand game, and common Vietnamese words and phrases that children can learn (along with the phrases they will absorb through the songs that they listen to and learn for themselves). Jessica Đinh's illustrations flavor the collection with delightful images of children, animals and traditional practices.

This is a beautiful compendium of children's expressive practices that sits at the well-springs of Vietnamese-American heritage. It has the capacity to open up all children to the joys and wonders of childhood at large, as well as to draw them into the specificity of an important American cultural community. It offers a journey into music, language, and traditional practices, and into the world of Vietnam that many Americans still refer to as their origin-place, a homeland, a vital place to which they trace their family traditions.

Patricia Shehan Campbell
University of Washington

Preface

The Vietnamese Children's Songbook is an introduction to the rich repertoire of Vietnamese children's songs and culture. I hope that this collection of songs will be useful to Vietnamese-American parents who are interested in ensuring these songs live on. This book will also be useful to anyone else interested in enjoying, teaching, and learning about Vietnamese heritage and music, including music educators, children, friends, and family members.

Vietnam is located on the eastern coast of Southeast Asia, bordering China to the north, and Laos and Cambodia to the west. It is often referred to as a "dragon-shaped" country. Its entire eastern coast lies against the South China Sea, with the Gulf of Tonkin to the north, and the Mekong Delta to the south. The songs chosen for this book are from the northern and southern regions of Vietnam. In the future, an additional volume that highlights the beauty of children's songs from Central Vietnam may be forthcoming.

The book is divided into two parts. The first part consists of children's songs. Each song includes musical notation, Vietnamese lyrics, an English translation, and is set within a colorful illustration which evokes the playfulness of childhood. A pronunciation guide for the Vietnamese language is included.

Scan the QR code to access digital downloads of song recordings, speaking tracks to learn lyrics phrase by phrase, and videos to watch native Vietnamese speakers pronounce the lyrics. Digital downloads are available for all songs in this book.

The second part of the book provides a glimpse into the cultural exuberance of Vietnamese childhood during the Mid-Autumn Harvest Moon Festival, in which mooncakes, lanterns, and games all play a part. An introductory guide of simple phrases for new learners of the Vietnamese language is also included along with audio examples. Scan the QR code to access digital downloads of the audio examples.

A teaching supplement is sold separately for music educators and is available as a PDF file only. This instructional tool offers suggestions and tips for teaching the songs and can be used for classrooms, studios, and community settings. *The Vietnamese Children's Songbook: Teacher's Guide* is available at FFlat-Books.com

The Vietnamese Children's Songbook serves as a resource for parents, educators, librarians, children, and enthusiasts who have the desire to learn and enjoy Vietnamese children's songs. It is a first glimpse into Vietnamese childhood and traditional delights, including songs, games, cultural practices, and language. I hope you enjoy this little journey and will join me for the journeys to come.

Tina A. Huỳnh
Tacoma, WA
2023

Please visit the accompanying website, https://www.vietchildrenssongs.com/. All songs are available on streaming platforms.

Vietnamese Pronunciation Guide

Hướng Dẫn Phát Âm

The Vietnamese national written language (quốc ngữ) is Latin-based. Below is a guide using the International Phonetic Alphabet and American English-equivalent sounds to help you pronounce the lyrics in the southern and northern Vietnamese dialects.

In Vietnamese, there are six tones that change the meaning of words:

Name of Diacritic	Diacritic, as written on the letter A	Description	International Phonetic Alphabet Symbol
Dấu ngang	A (none)	Level, unwavering	˧
Dấu sắc	Á (acute accent)	High, rising	˦
Dấu huyền	À (grave accent)	Low, falling	˨
Dấu hỏi	Ả (small hook above)	Low, falling then rising	˧˩˧
Dấu ngã	Ã (tilde)	High, creaky/broken	˧ˀ
Dấu nặng	Ạ (dot below)	Low, broken then rising	˧ˀ or ˨ˀ

The Vietnamese alphabet:

A a [æ] Between "rat" and "father"	Ă ă [ʌ] Between "rat" and "cut"	Â a [ʌ] As in "under"	B b [b] As in "bat"	C c [k] Between "cat" and "gut"	D d [j/z] Southern: "yet" Northern: "zipper"	Đ đ [d] As in "dark" but with a dental sound	E e [ɛ] As in "bet"	Ê ê [eI] As in "aim"	G g [ɣ] No English equivalent; like "amigo" in Spanish
H h [h] As in "hat"	I i [i] As in "eat"	K k [k] Between "cat" and "gut"	L l [l] As in "line"	M m [m] As in "mom"	N n [n] As in "not"	O o [ɔ] As in "on"	Ô ô [o] As in "or"	Ơ ơ [ʌ:] As in "under"	P p [p] As in "pot". Note: "ph" results in "f" as in "fawn"
Q q [k] As in "cat"	R r [ʒ/z] Southern: Similar to "measure" Northern: "zoo"	S s [ʃ/s] Southern: Similar to "shop" Northern: "sit"	T t [t/d] Between "tart" and "does"	U u [u] As in "oolong"	Ư ư [ɨ] No English equivalent; Between "is" and "under"	V v [j/v] Southern: "yet" Northern: "vet"	X x [s] As in "sit"	Y y [i:/ij] As in "ear"	

New sounds are formed when letters and diacritics are combined.

To see and hear examples of the songs as they are spoken and sung in Vietnamese, scan the QR code to access digital downloads of song recordings, speaking practice tracks, and videos.

Vietnamese Children's Songs

Click on the QR code below to access supplemental resources:

- Audio recordings of all songs
- Practice tracks for speaking the lyrics
- Videos for visual and aural guidance on speaking the lyrics

GOIN' FISHING

This evening I'm goin' fishing,
I'm bringing my trap
To catch some crab!
I'd better do well
So mom can cook some crab soup.
Oh! There's a crab!
Oh! There's a crab!
Shh, don't be loud!
Or it will crawl back down.
Don't be loud!
Or it will crawl back down.

Chiều Nay Em Đi Câu Cá

Traditional

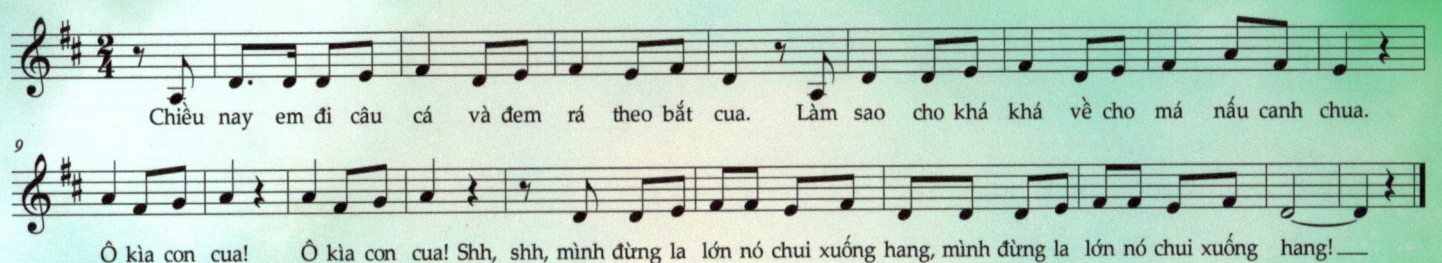

With Excitement

Chiều nay em đi câu cá và đem rá theo bắt cua. Làm sao cho khá khá về cho má nấu canh chua.

Ô kìa con cua! Ô kìa con cua! Shh, shh, mình đừng la lớn nó chui xuống hang, mình đừng la lớn nó chui xuống hang!

THE CAT

Kitty, kitty, climbing up the Areca palm,
Asking where mousie has gone.
Mousie has gone to the market,
To buy salted fish and salt
For kitty's father's funeral!

Con Mèo

Traditional

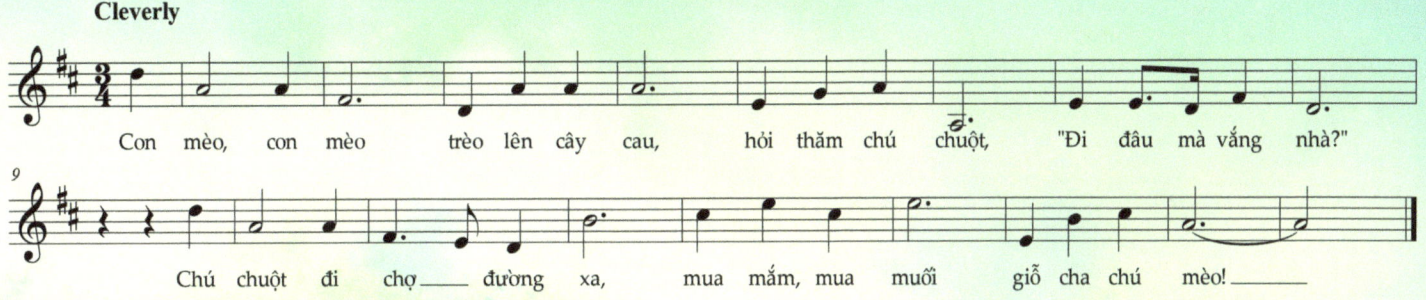

Cleverly

Con mèo, con mèo trèo lên cây cau, hỏi thăm chú chuột, "Đi đâu mà vắng nhà?"

Chú chuột đi chợ đường xa, mua mắm, mua muối giỗ cha chú mèo!

THE TOAD

Come out and look!
Something's sitting on the ground.
It's showing its back, it's a toad.
The toad sitting in the corner,
It's showing its back, it's a baby toad!

For more verses, visit vietchildrenssongs.com

Con Cóc (Ra Mà Xem)

Traditional

2nd verse	Ra mà xem, cái gì nó ngồi trong xó Nó đưa cái tai ra ngoài, đó là con chó Con chó nó ngồi trong xó Nó đưa cái tai ra ngoài Đó là chó con.	Come out and look! Something's sitting in the corner. It's showing its paw, it's a dog. The dog is sitting in the corner. It's showing its back, It's a puppy.
3rd verse	Ra mà xem, cái gì nó ngồi nó nghĩ Nó đưa cái đuôi ra ngoài, đó là con khỉ Con khỉ nó ngồi nó nghĩ Nó đưa cái đuôi ra ngoài Ấy là khỉ con	Come out and look! Something's sitting and thinking. It's showing its tail, it's a monkey. The monkey is sitting and thinking, It's showing its tail, It's a baby monkey.

YELLOW BUTTERFLY

Yellow butterfly
Yellow butterfly
Spread your wings
Spread your wings
Fly in circles three times
Fly in circles five times
I sit and watch
I sit and watch

Kìa Con Bướm Vàng

Traditional

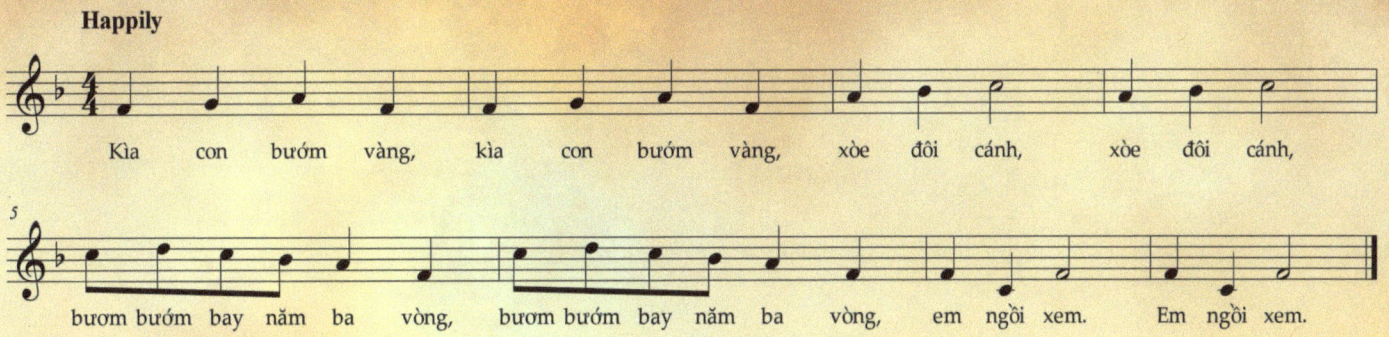

Happily
Kìa con bướm vàng, kìa con bướm vàng, xòe đôi cánh, xòe đôi cánh,
5
bươm bướm bay năm ba vòng, bươm bướm bay năm ba vòng, em ngồi xem. Em ngồi xem.

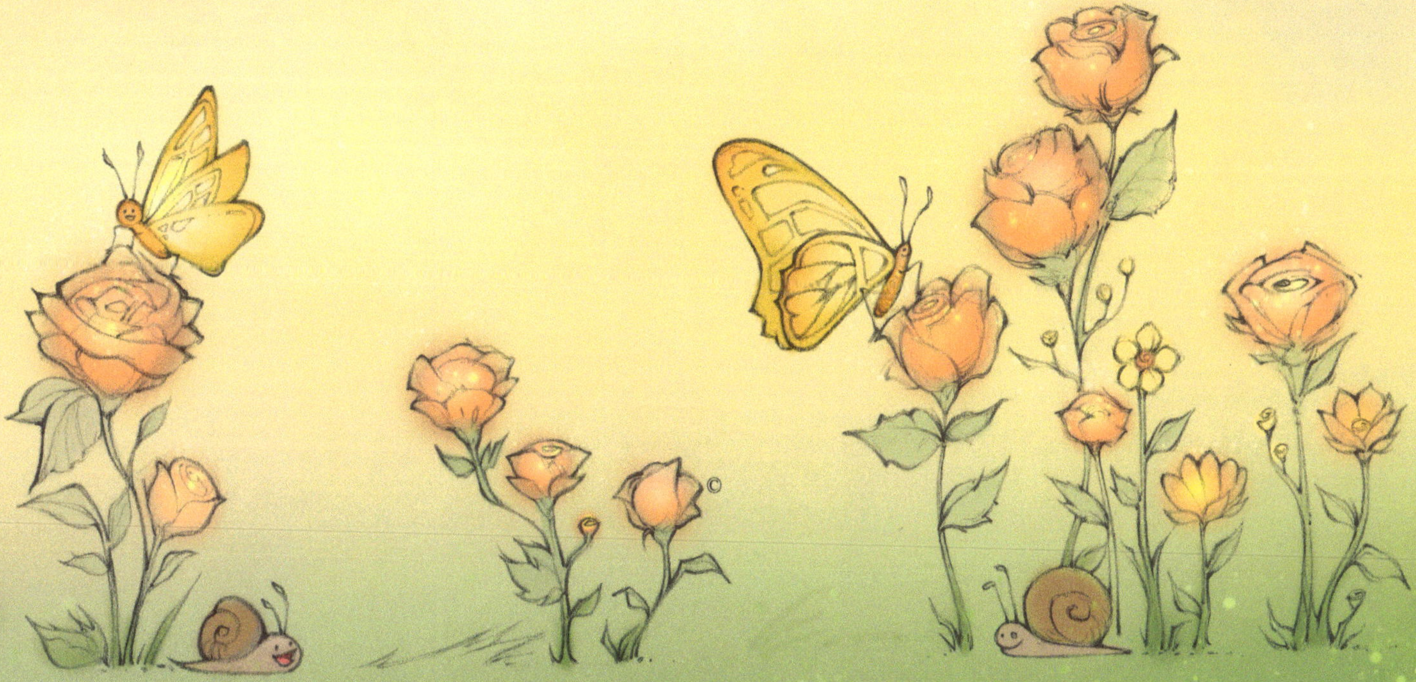

THE TWO LITTLE LIZARDS

Two little lizards
Playfully bit off each other's tails.
Daddy lizard was sad
He called them and scolded them.
Two little lizards
With big tails but they fell off.
Ow, how painful!
They cried so much!

Hai Con Thằn Lằn Con

Traditional

Teasing

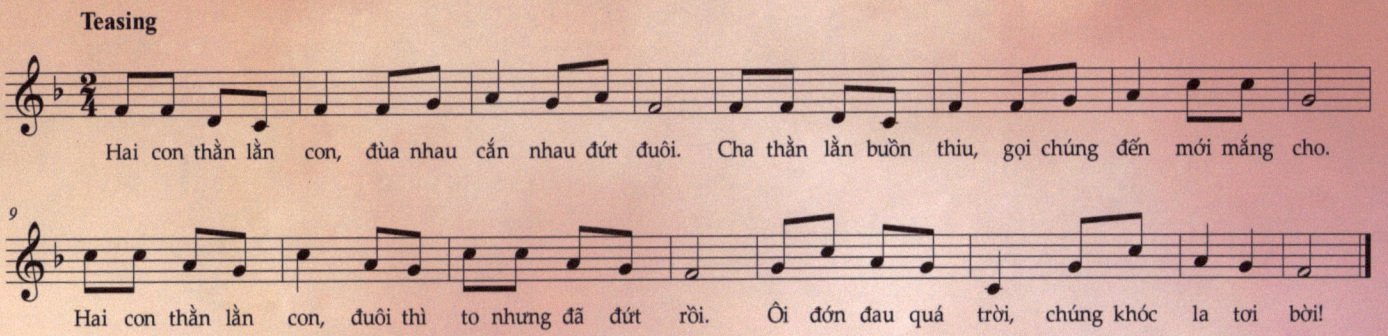

Hai con thằn lằn con, đùa nhau cắn nhau đứt đuôi. Cha thằn lằn buồn thiu, gọi chúng đến mắng cho.

Hai con thằn lằn con, đuôi thì to nhưng đã đứt rồi. Ôi đớn đau quá trời, chúng khóc la tơi bời!

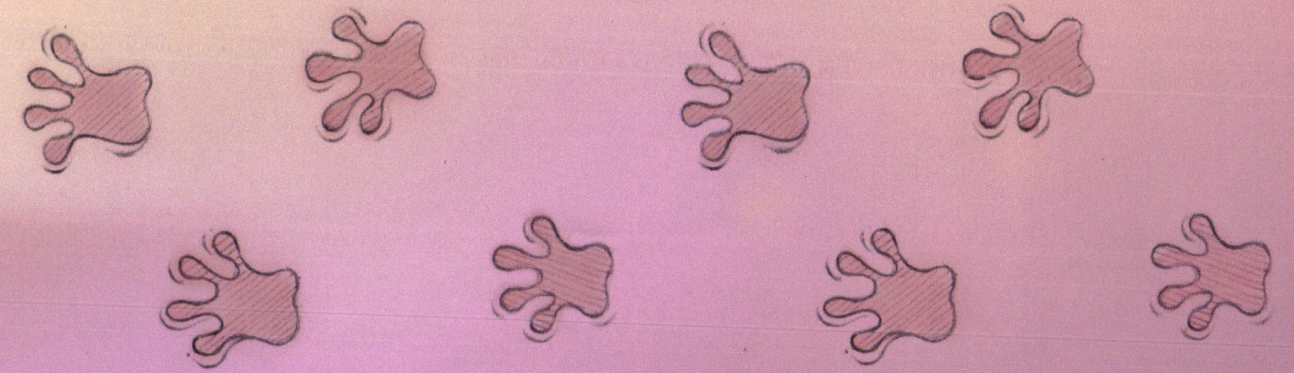

LOOK! THERE'S AN ELEPHANT

Let's look at the elephant! He is swaying,
Leaning near some spiders spinning webs.

Mr. Elephant is having such a great time,
So he invites another elephant to come play.

Trông Kìa Con Voi

Anonymous

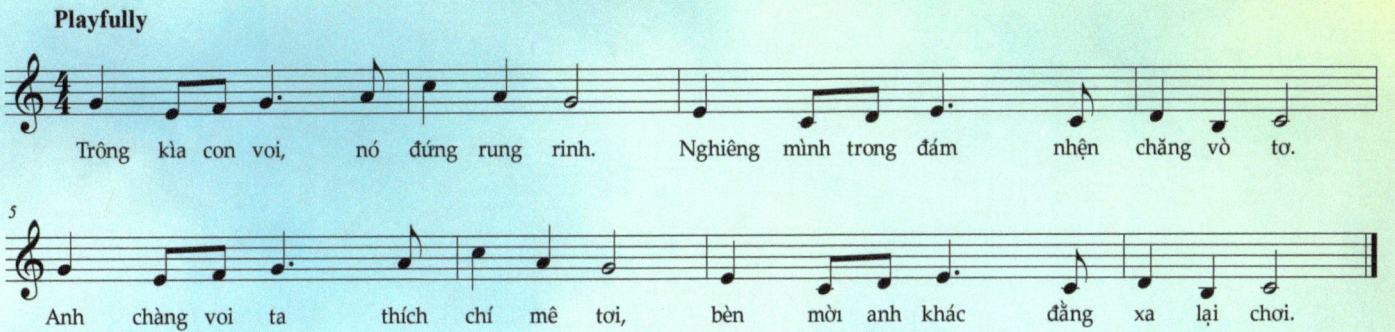

Playfully
Trông kìa con voi, nó đứng rung rinh. Nghiêng mình trong đám nhện chăng vò tơ.
5
Anh chàng voi ta thích chí mê tơi, bèn mời anh khác đằng xa lại chơi.

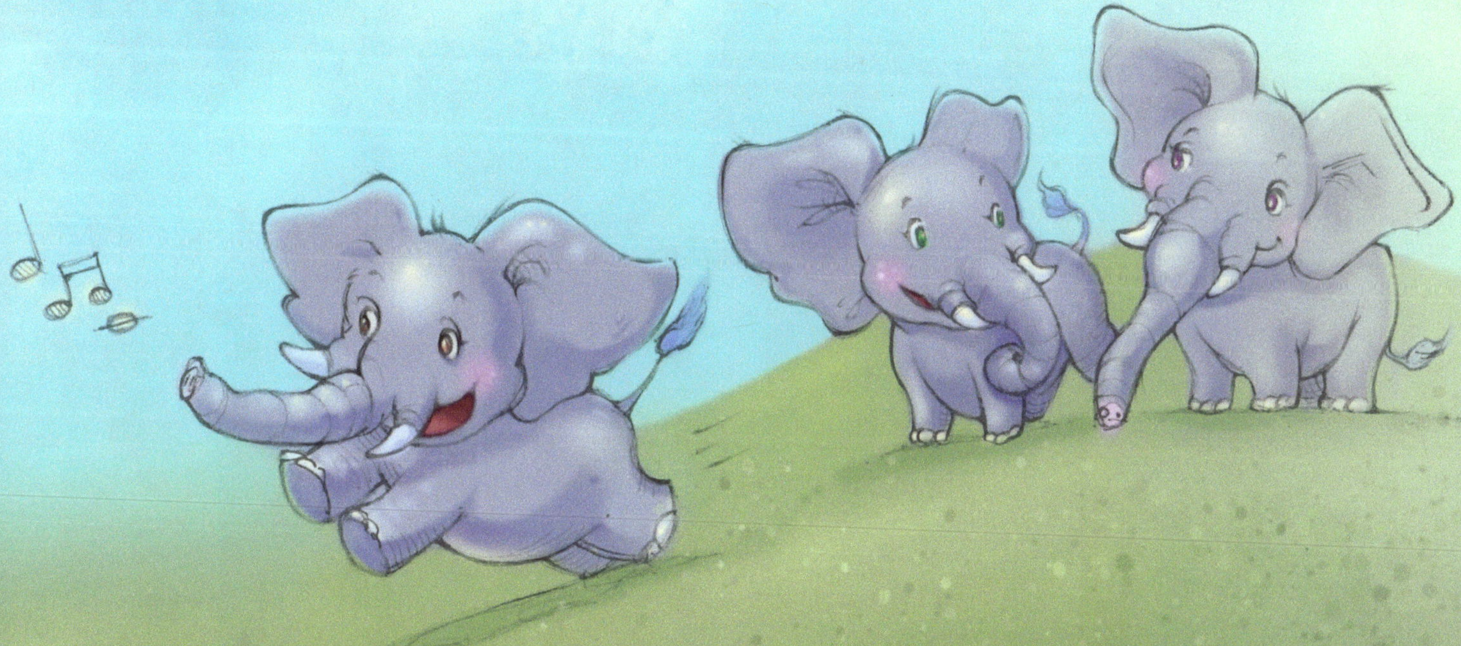

THE LITTLE STORK

The little stork
Perched on a bamboo branch
It left home, but didn't ask Mom,
Who knows where it went?
I ask for permission when I leave
I say hello when I come back
My little mouth is open
Do you love me, mom?

Mẹ Yêu Không Nào (Con Cò Bé Bé)

Lê Xuân Thọ

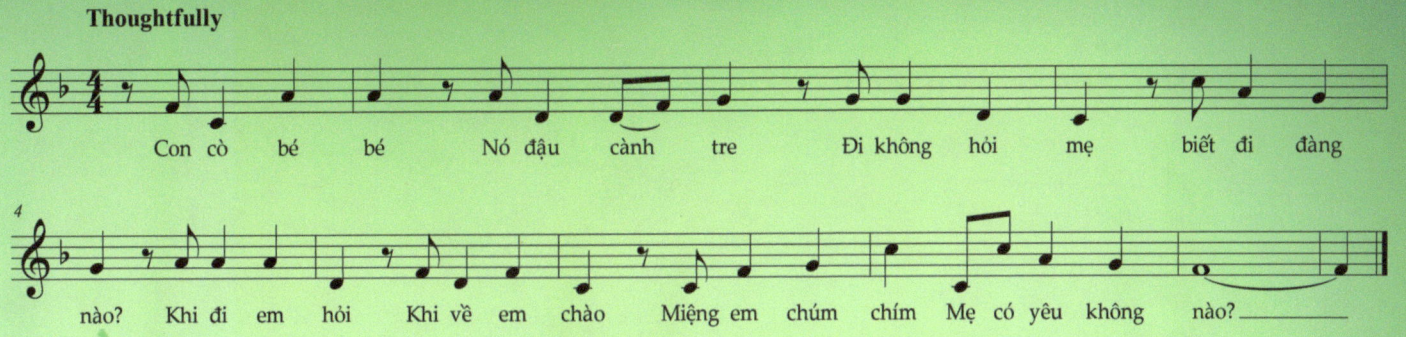

LET'S GET OUR AUGUST LANTERNS

At the Mid-Autumn festival, get your lanterns and go out,
I walk all around town with a lit lantern.
With a happy heart and lantern in hand,
I dance and sing to the autumn moon.

Star lantern, fish lantern,
Swan lantern, butterfly lantern.
Take my lantern to the moon!
Blue lantern, purple lantern,
Green lantern, white lantern,
All colors shimmering in the light.

For more verses, visit vietchildrenssongs.com

MY DAD AND MOM

In the early morning,
My dad goes to the rice fields to work,
My mom goes to the rice fields to work.
My dad is a farmer,
My mom is also a farmer.
Together we live in the vast rice fields.
Some nights when the full moon rises,
The wind and rain make the trees sound.
We get together and have fun
We get together and sing
In the shimmering ivory moonlight.
Come Harvest,
Come here to the immense fields.
Together we dance and sing in the rice fields.
Come, Peace. In life, we're ascending,
Shining bright like the moon's reflection on the water.

Cultural Treasures

There are many Vietnamese cultural traditions including holidays, food, games, and festivals. One festival is called "Tết Trung Thu", or the Mid-Autumn Harvest Moon Festival. This festival takes place during the full moon on the fifteenth day in the eighth month of the lunar calendar, usually in September or October. The full moon symbolizes wishes for a well-rounded life. For Vietnamese rice farmers, this full moon indicates the end of the rice harvest and a time to spend with family. Even though some Vietnamese do not harvest rice where they live, they still celebrate this event. Children participate in lantern parades, eat moon cakes, sing, dance, and play games. In the next section, you can learn more about these Vietnamese cultural treasures.

Mooncakes

Bánh Trung Thu

These special cakes are made just for Tết Trung Thu. Families give and receive these during the Mid-Autumn Harvest Moon Festival. Here are three different mooncakes - "bánh nướng", "bánh thập cẩm", and "bánh dẻo". Although they may contain different ingredients, all three mooncakes have beautiful designs imprinted on top.

Traditional Moon Cake

Bánh Nướng

"Bánh" means cake, and "nướng" means to bake. Chopped nuts, meats, and sometimes fruits are molded into a square shape and encased in a flour shell. Often, there is a salted, hard cooked egg yolk called "lòng đỏ trứng muối" inside, which symbolizes the moon. The baker brushes egg white on the outside which protects the shell and gives it some shine before putting it in the oven to bake. Some varieties of "bánh nướng" include "đậu xanh" with mung bean paste inside, "đậu đỏ" with red bean paste inside, or "hột sen" with lotus seeds inside.

Mixed Nuts Mooncake

Bánh Thập Cẩm

This mooncake can contain up to 10 varieties of chopped nuts and seeds packed together tightly in the mold of the cake. It may also have a salted, hard cooked egg yolk inside.

Sticky Rice Mooncake

Bánh Dẻo

"Dẻo" means soft and flexible, like the outside of this mooncake. Also known as Snow Skin Mooncake, it is made with a shell of sweet rice or "bột nếp" and can contain either red bean paste, called "đậu đỏ", or mung bean paste, called "đậu xanh". Sometimes it contains lotus seeds, called "hột sen", and sometimes there is no hard cooked egg yolk inside. This cake does not have to be baked.

Lanterns: How to Make a Lantern
Lồng Đèn

Under the glow of the full moon during the Harvest Moon Festival (Tết Trung Thu), children parade in the streets while carrying colorfully lit lanterns. There are many ways to make your own lantern. Ask an adult if you need help. Here is one fun and easy way!

Materials: Construction paper, hole puncher, scissors, tape, string, ribbon, 2 thin cardboard discs cut to be the same circumference as the length of your construction paper (use string to measure the length of the paper, and then shape the string into a circle to cut the discs).

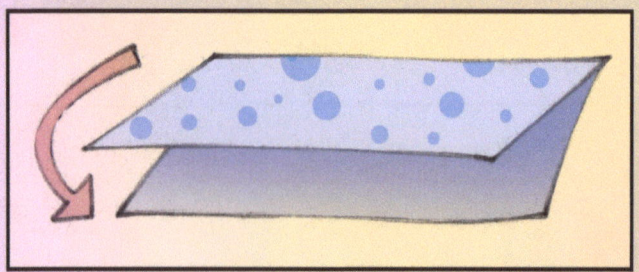

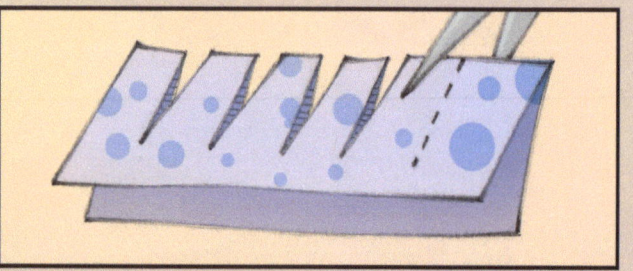

1. **Fold** a piece of construction paper in half lengthwise.

2. **Mark** light pencil lines every 3/4 inch along the folded edge, stopping about an inch from the bottom edge. **Cut** along the pencil lines. Remember to stop an inch before the edge of the paper.

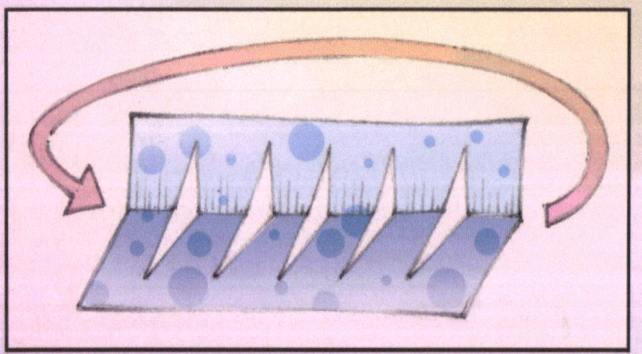

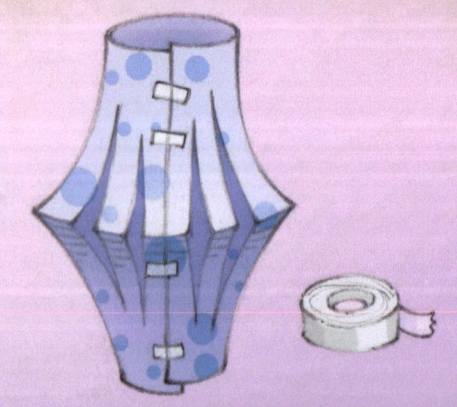

3. **Unfold** the sheet of construction paper and lay it flat. **Tape** the short edges together to make a cylinder as in the image to the right.

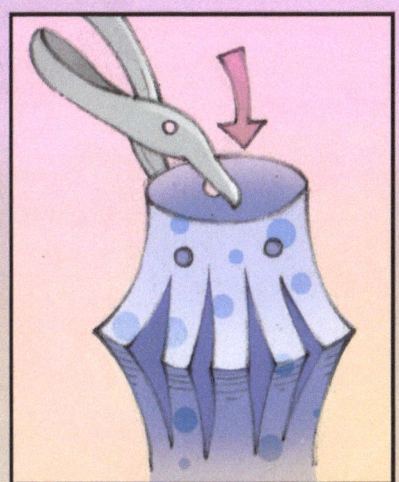

The finished lantern!

4. **Punch** 3 or 4 holes around both the top and bottom edges of the lantern.

5. **Attach** string to the holes on top and **tie** them together above the lantern.

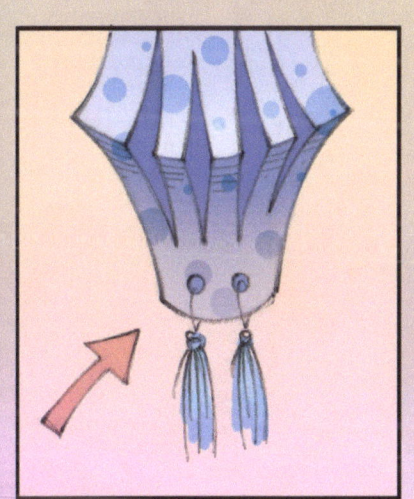

6. **Attach** tassels or ribbons to the holes on the bottom edge of the lantern.

7. Tape cardboard discs to the top and bottom of the lantern.

Tips:

You can experiment making different sized lanterns with various sizes of construction paper and various thickness of cuts. Make sure your disk sizes match the lantern body!

For a fun twist, use embroidery thread to make the tassels.

Add a battery-operated tea light inside the lantern to light it up!

Let's Play a Game!
Trò Chơi

In this game, a group of children gather around one person. That person holds out the palm of their hand while all the children place one finger in the person's palm. Everyone recites the rhyme below while the children bounce their finger on the palm to the steady beat of the rhyme. At the end of the rhyme on the word "ập", the person holding out their palm must try to grab any of the fingers in the palm. Whoever gets their finger caught by the palm is "out". The game may be repeated until there is one finger left (the winner). It may also be played so that whoever gets their finger caught first must be the next person to hold out their palm. This game may be played with as few as two people. All that is required is one person's finger and another person's palm.

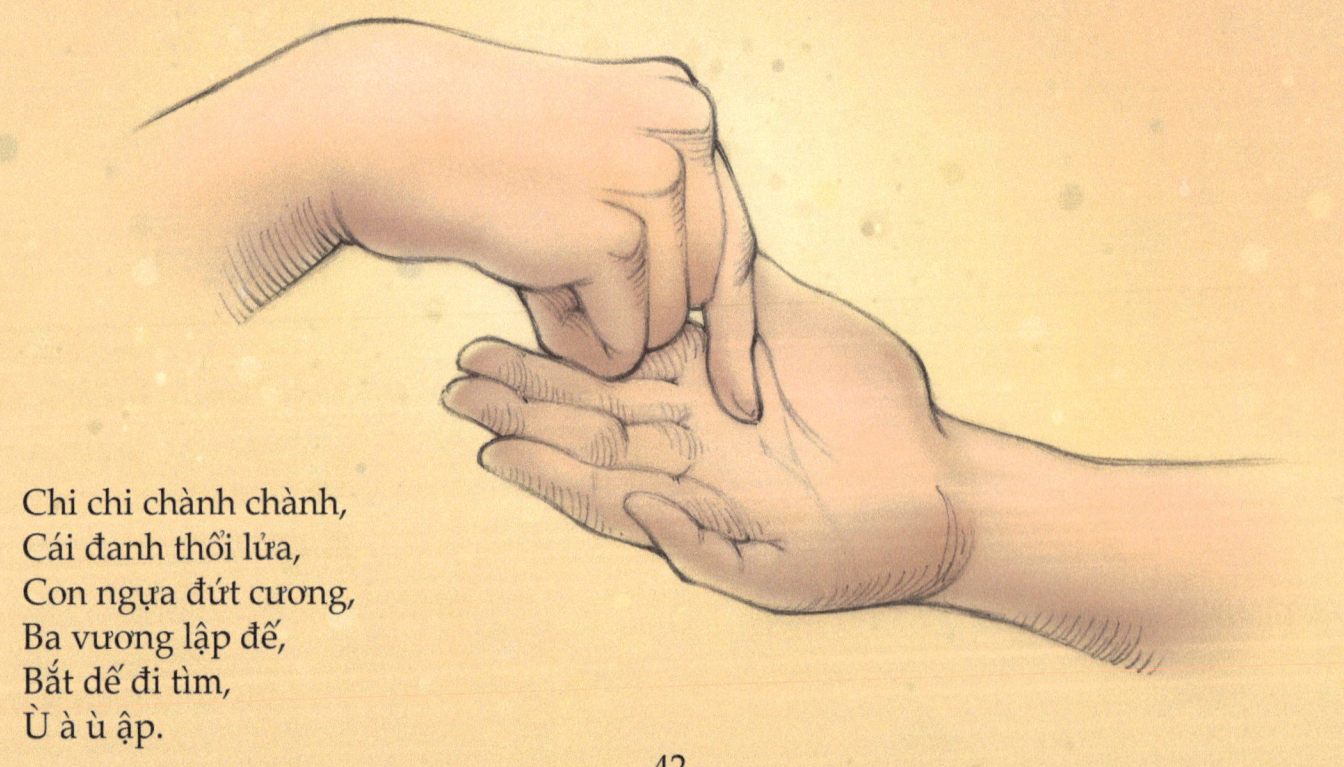

Chi chi chành chành,
Cái đanh thổi lửa,
Con ngựa đứt cương,
Ba vương lập đế,
Bắt dế đi tìm,
Ù à ù ập.

This rhyme contains words that have no real meaning, much like "tra la la" in English has no meaning. The combined phrases also have no overarching meaning, but are rhythmic and entertaining when combined. It is a silly rhyme, similar to The Cat and the Fiddle, in which cows jump over moons and dishes run away with spoons.

Chi chi chành chành,
The fire-blowing stick,
The horse's ropes break free,
Three princes crown a king,
Who tells the cricket to find the horse,
Ù à ù ập.

Let's Speak Vietnamese

Nói Tiếng Việt

In daily life there are common words and phrases that children use regularly. The phrases below are spoken from the child's point of view, using "em" to refer to the child. Use the Pronunciation Guide on pages 12-13 and access audio examples through the QR code to help you pronounce the words. Practice speaking with your friends!

Phrases

Hello ____! – Chào (name)!

How are you? – (Name) khỏe không?

I'm fine. – (Name) khỏe.

Goodbye, I'm going home! – Chào (name), em đi về.

Thank you – Cám ơn

You're welcome – Không có chi

What's your name? – Em tên là gì?

My name is – Em tên là (name).

Where do you live? – Em ở đâu?

I live in – Em ở (city).

People

Father – ba (south), bố (north)

Mother – má (south), mẹ (north)

Older sister or female a little older than you – chị

Older brother or male a little older than you – anh

Other ways to address people:

Em (someone younger than you, or yourself)

Cô (a female a bit older than you)

Chú (a male a bit older than you)

Bác (a female or male a lot older than you)

Bà (a woman as old as your grandmother)

Ông (a male as old as your grandfather)

About the Author

Tina A. Huỳnh is a music educator with over 20 years of experience teaching general music, instrumental and choral music in private, public, and studio settings. She discovered a love for music at a young age through the Vietnamese songs her parents used to sing to her, such as "Con Mèo" and "Trông Kìa Con Voi", as well as American children's music books with accompaniment tapes such as the Wee Sing series. Beginning piano lessons at age six, she later learned the flute and saxophone. Tina earned a Bachelor of Music degree in Music Education, Bachelor of Arts in French and California Teaching Credential in K-12 Music from California State University Long Beach, and Master of Music and Doctor of Musical Arts degrees in Music Education from the University of Southern California. Tina is currently Assistant Professor of Music Education at the University of Puget Sound in Tacoma, WA. Tinaahuynh.com

About the Illustrator

Jessica Đinh was first drawn to art by the numerous books her parents would read to her as a child, from bright and colorful picture books to illustrated novels, such as *The Hobbit* by J.R.R. Tolkien. She earned a Bachelor of Fine Arts degree from Laguna College of Art and Design and has a passion for both art and music, having played the piano for over 20 years. As a first generation Vietnamese American, Jessica finds special meaning in this project as she endeavors to preserve her heritage and share it with others through her artwork in this book.

About the Contributing Artists

Vocals | Bích-Vân Nguyễn, singer-actress-songwriter, producer and TV host has performed in Opera, Musical Theater and stage productions, headlining concerts at Kennedy Center, Rainbow Room (Rockefeller Center), Segerstrom Center for the Arts, Musco Center for the Arts… and internationally. She recently performed the lead role of Mai in the world-premiere of the opera "What the Horse Eats".
www.bichvanofficial.com

Guitar | Minh Nguyễn is a Vietnamese guitarist. His skill and talent brought him to the United States to study guitar at the University of Wisconsin-Milwaukee, University of Puget Sound, and University of Southern California. He performs a wide variety of styles. His focus on classical guitar earned him first prize in the 2014 Sierra Nevada Guitar Competition, among other competitions.

Percussion | Jimmy Trần is a Vietnamese-American composer, drummer, percussionist, and educator. He is well-versed with jazz, Latin, indie, and popular music styles. He has toured internationally and regularly performs with Tini Grey, Loa Greyson, and other bands. He was featured in Modern Drummer Magazine's April 2018 issue and is the author of *Mr. Tinyjam's Play-along Rock "Hits" for Drummers*.
www.mrtinyjammusic.com

Producer | Todd Heinrich is a Los Angeles-based producer, songwriter, musician, and studio manager at a major television network. His passion and knowledge about many cultures is rooted in a dedication to preserving World Music.

Audio Recording Credits

Vocals: Bích-Vân Nguyễn
Guitar: Minh Nguyễn
Flute, Piccolo, & Slide Whistle: Tina A. Huỳnh
Percussion: Jimmy Trần, Tina A. Huỳnh, and Todd Heinrich

Produced by Todd Heinrich and Tina A. Huỳnh

All songs arranged by Tina A. Huỳnh, Minh Nguyễn, and Todd Heinrich

Recorded, mixed and mastered by Todd Heinrich July - August 2016 and June 2017 at TomorrowLabs, Los Angeles, California, United States

Video Recording Credits

A special thanks goes to the children who contributed videos to this book. You make the book extra special! Thanks to the parents for allowing them to be a part of this project.

Audio Recording Track List

> Scan the QR code to access all tracks and accompanying videos.

Song 1:
    Track 1 - Goin' Fishing – Chiều Nay Em Đi Câu Cá
    Track 2 - Pronunciation

Song 2:
    Track 3 - The Cat – Con Mèo
    Track 4 - Pronunciation

Song 3:
    Track 5 - The Toad – Con Cóc
    Track 6 - Pronunciation

Song 4:
    Track 7 - Counting Stars – Đếm Sao
    Track 8 - Pronunciation

Song 5:
    Track 9 - Yellow Butterfly – Kìa Con Bướm Vàng
    Track 10 - Pronunciation

Song 6:
    Track 11 - The Two Little Lizards – Hai Con Thằn Lằn Con
    Track 12 - Pronunciation

Song 7:
    Track 13 - Look! There's An Elephant – Trong Kìa Con Voi
    Track 14 - Pronunciation

Song 8:
    Track 15 - The Little Stork – Con Cò Bé Bé
    Track 16 - Pronunciation

Song 9:
    Track 17 - Let's Get Our August Lanterns – Rước Đèn Tháng Tám
    Track 18 - Pronunciation

Song 10:
    Track 19 - Dad and Mom in the Rice Fields – Tía Má Em
    Track 20 - Pronunciation

Let's Speak Vietnamese:
    Track 21 - Phrases
    Track 22 - People
    Track 23 - Other Ways to Address People

www.ingramcontent.com/pod-product-compliance
Lightning Source LLC
Chambersburg PA
CBHW041520070526
44585CB00002B/25